Chapter One

INTRODUCTION

If you are reading this, then you know that you or someone you love is making poor sexual choices or feel that their sexual behavior is out of control. People who are impulsive sexually often find that they experience an "addiction" to sex similar to drug addiction. Sexual addiction is a very real problem that often brings negative consequences. The ability to resolve sexual addiction becomes a vicious cycle in which you participate in negative behavior despite these consequences.

Not everyone sees their behavior as a problem needing resolution. However, if you read the steps in this book you can become clearer on how poor choices lead to negative sexual behavior. These behaviors often affect relationships, work, family obligations, occupational goals, and even your own sense of self. Only you know if your sexual behavior has become a negative force in your life. You may experience negative sexual behavior that leads to taking advantage of situations or people in order to satisfy your own needs. Reasons for reading about such behavior is that you can clarify the choices you are making and decide if they are harmful enough to qualify for a sexual addiction. It can be helpful to learn more about when and why you manipulate, coerce or otherwise gain control of sexual situations. A sign of addiction often includes exploiting others who trust you! It is crucial then to understand how your addictive lifestyle is affecting other parts of your life. With sexual addiction, often you are having negative consequences in many areas but choose to ignore them. Or you want to stop a particular practice and find yourself not being able to do so. Addictions dominate your sexual behavior and often become more and more intrusive in other parts of your life. Your "baggage" blocks the ability to have honest and open relationships. Being secretive, or living a life that you have to keep secret, is an indication that sexual addiction may be present and interfering with your ability to maintain a relationship that allows others to be close to you. Often people participate in the behaviors of sexual addiction but become very secretive and do not wish to see the impact secrecy has on all parts of your life. This can lead to denial and justification for why your relationships are not working. With any addiction, a person may try to rid themselves of negative sexual thinking but fail to manage or eliminate this behavior and thinking.   An ability to examine your sexual behavior and welcome change becomes more comfortable as you begin to adjust your thinking. In changing your thinking, you begin to develop relationships where there is a give and take.   In promoting negative sexual behavior, you also promote relationships that are built on deceit. Now is a good time to identify shame and realistically look at your behavior. Unfortunately, shame often blocks change!   Sexual practices can then result in dishonesty. You can change your behavior but it takes knowledge and motivation. You may have now realized there is a problem but you have not been able to stop the harmful behavior. The need for positive sexual decisions can occur at any time in one's life. You are reading this book for a reason!   If you follow steps towards accountability and a willingness to change then you may be more successful in eliminating destructive sexual thinking.

SEXUALLY COMPULSIVE BEHAVIOR AND IMPULSIVE SEXUAL BEHAVIOR ARE VERY SIMILAR BECAUSE THEY CONTINUE TO OCCUR REGARDLESS OF THE CONSEQUENCES. COMPULSIVE BEHAVIOR HAS NEGATIVE REPERCUSSIONS AND IS A BEHAVIOR OCCURING OVER AND OVER. IMPULSIVE BEHAVIOR IS THE ABILITY TO ENGAGE IN POSITIVE OR NEGATIVE BEHAVIOR DESPITE ITS NEGATIVE CONSEQUENCES. BOTH TYPES OF SEXUAL BEHAVIOR HAVE NEGATIVE IMPACTS ON YOUR LIFE ESPECIALLY IN THE AREA OF RELATIONSHIPS. COMPULSIVE BEHAVIOR AND IMPULSIVE BEHAVIOR OFTEN EXIST TOGETHER. NOW IS THE TIME TO TAKE A CAREFUL LOOK AT THE CONSEQUENCES OF YOUR BEHAVIOR. DO NOT GET CAUGHT UP IN THE LABEL OF SEXUAL ADDICTION. YOU ARE SEEKING CHANGE AND CHANGE ALONE. START NOW TO ADDRESS YOUR THINKING AND SEE HOW THIS HAS AFFECTED YOUR BEHAVIOR.

If you are engaging in behaviors that are affecting negatively other areas of your life, then this suggests a need to address these behaviors.   You may have identified the impact of your sexual behavior on other areas of your life but have not resolved the behavior. For instance, if you are engaging in random sexual encounters this eventually negatively impacts your self worth and guilt as you have learned to use others for your own self gratification. Anyone can change their thinking if they learn to not give in to urges leading to negative behavior. The time to change is now! You can achieve the same gratification by having healthy sexual encounters.

You must first decide whether you feel that your sexual behavior is negative and not conducive to healthy relationships. One person's view of negative behavior may be viewed quite differently by someone else. You have to decide how a behavior is affecting your life. Only you can decide if a behavior is something you wish to change. Often a person will not view their negative behavior as needing change unless they encounter emotional consequences. You must decide when to change and why. You must decide whether eliminating this behavior is worth the effort in changing it. Many times addressing negative sexual behavior can be difficult because intense emotions such as shame and embarrassment block change. You are the sole decision maker in deciding if change is necessary. You can with effort dedicate yourself to being a positive sexual being! Change is difficult but more rewarding than continuing to engage in behavior that has negative consequences in your life!

Sexually appropriate behavior should never include exploiting another person. You should never have to manipulate or exploit another person to be sexually satisfied. If you must coerce, manipulate, or use another person than this behavior is not typical of healthy sexual choices. The wellbeing of others should never be affected by your choices. Sometimes you will have continued these sexual behaviors over many years and you considered your behavior as less than damaging. You can always start making positive choices for whatever reasons you have chosen to come to this book!

To better decide if this information applies to you, ask the question "Does your sexual conduct negatively affect yourself or others? If you can genuinely admit that the answer is yes than you need to evaluate your choices and change the mentality that leads to negative choices. Start here!!

You have the ability to change your thinking if you can honestly address the sexual behavior and the harm this behavior is creating for you. Decide if this material is helpful because you have searched your soul for honest answers and the ability to apply yourself to these strategies but change has not occurred. USE THE QUESTIONS AT THE TIME OF EACH CHAPTER TO FOCUS ON HOW THESE CHAPTERS RELATE TO YOU SPECIFICALLY.

Chapter Two

ARE YOU A SEX OFFENDER OR A SEXUAL ADDICT?

A negative sexual behavior comes with identifying your thinking and what leads to this behavior. The legal definition of a sex offender is anyone convicted of sexual behavior that is illegal in nature. These behaviors can include having sexual interactions with children or viewing child pornography. Other behaviors may include rape and sexual assault. A sex offender is anyone engaged in these behaviors and identified by the legal system. A sex offender has been convicted of sexual behavior considered illegal whether this behavior is executed once or a hundred times. This term includes the illegal behavior of a crime considered sexual in nature. This can include sexual acts towards children or exploiting another's vulnerability. A sex offender usually registers in a database provided by the legal system.

In the case of a sexual addict, there must be behaviors that you are not able to control (and resemble drug addiction). Any behavior that has produced negative consequences associated with your sexual behavior is termed a sexual addiction. Sexual addictions include indulging in a negative or repetitive behavior that you cannot control or change. You continue to participate in this behavior even though the consequences are either possible or present. You may have tried many times to quit but have not accomplished this on your own. Sexually negative behavior can include but is not limited to compulsive masturbation, sex with inappropriate partners, lengthy use of pornography, coercing children or adults to have sexual situations they would not normally consider, or using relationships that include sexual situations that only benefit you. Like any addiction, you continue to behave the exact same way each time but expect different results. There are many more behaviors considered to be addictive in the area of sexually inappropriate behavior. The cycle of addiction is present by ignoring the consequences or continuing a behavior that is negative in nature.

The behavior becomes more and more frequent. Often the addict is unable to resolve this behavior even with multiple attempts to do so.

Let's for our purposes here broaden the definition of sexual addiction to include any sexual behavior that is not typical or exploits another person but cannot be stopped by the person committing the act. If you have a sexual behavior that is not culturally acceptable and leads to negative relationships then you may suffer from a sexual addiction. In the case of a sexual addict, we include any behavior that continues to exist despite such negative consequences. This sexual behavior can be performed over and over despite your efforts to change. For instance, your viewing child pornography is at first exciting but at a certain point you see the damage of this activity and the harm done to these children. However you continue to view and masturbate to child pornography even after you have accepted the impact of this behavior. The same can be said about other damaging behaviors. Guilt does not stop the participation in this activity nor does feeling embarrassed each time. The feelings such as embarrassment or guilt are often ignored so the behavior can continue. This cycle is sexual addiction.

Behaviors can be less serious as viewing child pornography but are equally as destructive. Addictive behaviors are repetitive in nature and the extent of its harm is not the question. What is important in that this behavior is that you are unwilling or unable to discontinue this behavior. The compulsion is more intense than the thought about consequences. An addiction is anything that continues to harm you or others outside of you but exists despite the impact on others (or yourself). Sexual addiction is both compulsive (occurs over and over) and impulsive (inability to stop this behavior). Another example of sexual addiction and possibly more common is the need to include sexual partners that one does not know or engaging in sexual relationships as a result of social media. The internet has offered sexual addicts the chance to meet multiple random partners for sexual encounters. Sexual addiction often includes partners that one does not know and the addict can prey on people seeking a relationship. Social media has allowed people to form brief and often dysfunctional relationships online. These internet conversations can allow an addict to meet a person who is interested in a relationship and use them for a brief sexual encounter. Internet web sites can increase a sexual addiction in providing brief and nameless sexual encounters for the addict. This sexually inappropriate behavior can result in such consequences as the inability to form healthy relationships, harm to others whether physical or emotional, loss of employment, shame, emotional distress, and feelings of guilt. This is the cycle of a sexual addict. The internet increases one's ability to meet people and exploit them. It would be best if experiencing sexual addiction to not use the internet for any reason.

Sex should be pleasurable to you and your partner. If it is not, then you should ask yourself why this is not the case. If you are in a relationship, then you should ask yourself if this is a healthy and mutually pleasurable experience. You should not have to coerce or manipulate a partner to participate in sexual behavior that is acceptable only to you. This is another example of sexual addiction. An addiction negatively affects others in your life as well. Healthy sexual behavior is mutually beneficial. Sexual addiction focuses on the addict at the exclusion of everyone else. This is a huge red flag and needs to be identified and changed.

Typical sexual activity does not harm anyone! If your sexual urges or tastes extend to harming others or have potential to harm or exploit others then you may have a sexual addiction. This does not mean that you are less of a person or that you are a "bad guy". It does indicate that you could benefit from addressing behavior that has been an issue possibly for years. You can identify ways to change this behavior before you experience consequences that may or may not include negative relationships or legal issues! The road to recovery first starts with admitting there is a problem and having the motivation to change this behavior. With determination comes change and possibly healthier interactions with others.

You can't change what you don't admit! People are hesitant to embrace a negative label but it doesn't go away by wishing. You may need to accept that your behavior has become compulsive and harmful to yourself or others. With knowledge comes resolutions. The only way to change a behavior is to admit that you are part of this group called sexual addicts or sexual offenders. Otherwise there will continue to be excuses for why you don't have to change. Remember that you may be a person that is making poor sexual decisions but these choices only continue because you choose to participate in a cycle of addiction. First you must acknowledge these behaviors, expand your definition of what sexual addiction is, and seek the steps to better control the choices you make. This book is your first step. You must accept that you need to change and why. Many people embrace the idea that they are a bad person and this leads to resistance. The process of change has to start with you wanting to make other choices. Then you must educate yourself (and possibly require therapy). Additionally, you must approach change with honesty and a genuine need to examine your choices. You are solely responsible for your behavior and whether it changes or not is completely up to you. You decide if you are ready for long term change. You have to first decide if your behavior is out of control and whether it is beneficial to learn other ways to experience sexual pleasure. Then educate yourself on why you behave negatively and how this results in shame and embarrassment. Shame is usually an indication that behavior is not positive but rather something that is a result of exploitive sexual behavior. Shame is not the result of healthy choices that form positive relationships.

- ANSWER THE FOLLOWING TO BETTER HELP YOUR PROCESS :
- WHAT IS YOUR DEFINITION OF A SEX OFFENDER?
- WHAT IS YOUR DEFINITION OF SEXUAL ADDICTION?
- WHAT BEHAVIORS ARE YOU WILLING TO CHANGE?
- WHAT STEPS ARE YOU WILLING TO TAKE IN CHANGING YOUR PERSPECTIVE ABOUT YOUR SEXUAL BEHAVIOR ?
- DO YOU GENUINELY BELIEVE THAT YOU ARE PART OF THIS GROUP AND WHY?

Chapter Three

WHY I NEED TO CHANGE

If you are reading this book, then you suspect that you have issues relating to sexual choices. You need to decide if your behavior is a problem. Do this first for yourself. If you believe or know that your behavior is harmful then change may begin.

If you have decided your sexual choices are destructive then you know that changes have to be made. There are factors that cloud someone's desire to change and this is often a problem when dealing with sexual choices. Reasons for not embracing change is : change is often scary, you do not feel your behaviors are inclusive of people considered to having a sexual addiction, you believe you are not completely responsible for your sexual decisions, you have not suffered any legal consequences as a result of your sexual behavior, you are not really harming anyone by engaging in less than normal sexual behavior, your partner has not complained about acts that you engage in because she/he wants to please you, no one has commented on behavior that you have asked them to participate in, or you just want to live your life without changing for anyone (including yourself) and you don't wish to change. You should not postpone positive change for any reason.

You first need to decide if you have sexual behavior that is negative or harmful. If your behavior damages other's self esteem or you are unable to manage a healthy relationship due to your sexual behavior then you should consider change. If your choices are negatively impacting your own life or are negatively impacting others in your life, then you should want to address the impact of your sexual choices so that you can learn to participate in relationships that benefit both you and your partner. If you are changing for others, this will affect your ability to change your thinking process. Changing for others often does not lead to success. Others may want you to change but only with knowledge and will power can you change. You have to identify that there is a problem and you have the desire to change this behavior. The reality is that you can only achieve change when change is FOR YOU! Is this the time to change your own thinking and live a life where you have positive and healthy relationships or is the pleasure derived from unhealthy choices more desirable.

Another term for your behavior is "sexually destructive". This behavior also is about your own negative thinking and how you focus on yourself to fulfill your sexual needs. Whether your thinking is destructive or part of an addiction, the need for change has to come from you. Your destructive sexual thinking affects how you see your behavior. The focus on the well being of others is often not a consideration.   Your behavior considered to be addictive can include the following: excessive time spend participating in this behavior at the expense of other responsibilities, negative consequences due to this behavior and continuing to participate in this behavior anyway, failing on your own to try to eliminate this behavior, strong negative emotions when participating in this behavior, feelings such as denial or guilt surrounding your behavior. These behaviors become a part of your life without regard for physical, legal, financial, or emotional consequences. The cycle of destructive behavior includes some or all of these repercussions but the behavior continues to exist.

Sexual behavior that is destructive or impulsive often continues because someone is not convinced that the behavior is negatively affecting them or they have not reached "rock bottom" (yet). As with drugs, you don't believe that your life is suffering due to your sexual behavior or you just do not want to stop. The enjoyment is greater than the consequences. The reality is that everyone eventually suffers some kind of consequences for behavior that is truly destructive. Even small negative consequences become evident in the presence of this behavior. You may be caught up in the momentary pleasure rather than the impact your behavior. However the repercussions often include: a need to lie, being deceitful, feeling guilty, failure to stop your behavior, shame, financial burdens, destruction of relationships that were at one time healthy, and compulsive behavior such as excessive masturbation or exploiting others for the sake of your own pleasure.   You become the center of this world and you ignore what others' need or want. Everything and everyone else comes second!   The consequences of one's behavior becomes secondary to the enjoyment or compulsive nature of one's behavior. You have to decide if you are experiencing consequences as a result of your negative sexual thinking and honestly evaluate whether your behavior is harmful to others or yourself. Only then can someone successfully embark on change.

You have to be honest with yourself if you truly want to become a person able to make responsible and positive sexual choices. YOU have to decide how destructive your behaviors are and if YOU are ready to eliminate your "addiction" before you experience any further consequences. When you embrace change then the steps necessary to achieve this begin to make sense. With this new outlook, you can outline the necessity for change. The ability to change starts with the recognition that your sexual behavior benefits no one but you. You should not be a prisoner of your own sexual habits but rather released from the bonds that accompany sexually destructive choices.

- WHAT IS THE SEXUAL BEHAVIOR YOU WOULD LIKE TO CHANGE?
- WHAT HAVE BEEN THE CONSEQUENCES OF CONTINUING THIS BEHAVIOR?
- WHY ARE YOUR REASONS FOR WANTING TO CHANGE?
- WHAT WOULD BE THE BENEFIT OF CHANGING?

Chapter Four

SEXUAL TRAUMA

The issue of whether there is a high incidence of sexual abuse among those with sexual addiction has been a question for many years. Experts claim both that trauma is more common in sexual abusers and others claim that there is no greater chance of trauma in those with sexually inappropriate behavior. This issue I believe will never be resolved and researchers will always disagree on the impact of sexual abuse. Additionally, male survivors often do not tell out of embarrassment and this affects how we see trauma and later sexual behavior. The impact of sexual abuse and sexually impulsive behavior is not known.

In addition, we do know that sexual abuse as a whole is underreported to say the least. Instead of joining the fight against trauma, survivors especially boys do not want their secrets exposed especially in a court room full of people. The gravity of being a victim is often so unpleasant and most crimes go unreported.

If you are a sexual abuse survivor then you have additional work to do. You have experienced shame for some time and this complicates negative sexual behavior. It is important for you to not minimize your shame regarding your own abuse as you slowly look at your own trauma. It is easier to start with a firm foundation when you admit and work towards no longer being a victim. There are counselors and endless literature on surviving sexual abuse. This is a painful process but adequately explored may help you understand your own thinking.

There is no easy way to say if and how the sexual trauma affected your sexual thinking. It is often very evident that abuse leaves a wounded soul. Resolving this trauma while working on your own sexual behavior is a long process which must progress from shame to a stronger sense of self.

It is often overwhelming for someone to embrace the idea that you were abused and then abused someone else. One does not cause the other but it is very helpful to acknowledge old trauma so that you can eventually be a healthy trauma survivor.

You first have to accept that shame runs rampant in both situations and this is a very real barrier to change. You first have to accept that your trauma was not your fault and that your abuser damaged your thinking and sense of self worth. Find literature supporting a healthier prospective on being a survivor and work towards resolving this trauma.

Experts will never agree on the issue of sexual trauma in those with poor choices. You should consider how your own trauma affects your sexual beliefs. You are the only person to know whether your trauma will be a barrier to change. It does not have to be.

- ADMIT TO TRAUMA EVEN IF THIS JUST TO YOURSELF
- HOW DO YOU THINK THE TRAUMA HAS AFFECTED YOUR SEXUAL CHOICES.
- DO YOU NEED SUPPORT AND THERAPY FOR THIS EVENT IN YOUR LIFE.

Chapter Five

CYCLE OF ADDICTION

Sexual addiction is very much like drug addiction. You have lost control of your behavior and have possibly failed when addressing this on your own. At times, you feel overwhelmed and the sexual behavior seems out of control. Any addiction has periods where the behavior has become too frequent and too destructive! These sexual behaviors follow that same model. You have times where you feel that you can manage this behavior but this is seldom the case. Sexual addictions often have the same qualities. For instance, someone experiencing sexual addiction may feel that they are a slave to such behavior or thoughts. In your history, you have often relapsed even when you have tried abandoning your behavior. The negative consequences do not allow you to stop even when feeling shame. The addictive behavior continues to become more and more frequent. This behavior may even escalate to other behaviors more severe and more damaging. Identifying the destructive behavior is the key to achieving positive change. Negative behavior is no longer off limits! You need the same sexual gratification and you are less selective in how you achieve this. You have to initiate new behavior so that you can feel the thrill once evident in your early behavior. In addition, what is almost always present in sexual addiction is your failing to discontinue a behavior over time. Many fail at this because they don't have the knowledge to stop whatever is keeping them addicted. With a lack of knowledge in how to be sexually healthy, your relationships now include secrecy, denial or justifying your actions. You find yourself making excuses for why you cannot eliminate this thinking. You have lost sight of how damaging this behavior has become. This allows your negative sexual thinking to continue and to maintain a grasp on how you achieve sexual satisfaction. Your knowledge is the beginning of releasing yourself from sexual behavior that is often unhealthy.

As with sexual addiction and drug addiction, a person often has failed at trying to stop this behavior and the consequences have become more frequent and more severe. Often a person gives into the behavior and continues to ignore such consequences. The consequences are an afterthought that one does not acknowledge and the behavior gives only brief satisfaction. Immediate gratification becomes the person's complete focus. The addict knows the consequences and continues the behavior anyway so that he can gain momentary satisfaction. Negative emotions become more and more an issue and can include secrecy, shame and denial. The addict hides behind his addiction and nothing changes. Instead of eliminating the behavior these emotions often cause it to continue. The addict looks for sexual satisfaction but the consequences can become enormous. Even than the addict is a slave to his desires and he continues to engage in behavior that is harmful to oneself or others.

Addicts often refuse to reach out for help because the shame and embarrassment among other factors lead them to feeling exposed. The desire to enjoy the behavior and the impact of embarrassment feeds one's desire to continue their negative thinking. The behavior becomes exciting and the consequences have less of an impact because the pleasure is worth more than the desire to change.

It is often quite common for sexual addicts to have other substance abuse problems. This is because the mind of an addict is often open to exploiting substances as they do unhealthy sexual behavior. The mind is open to violating one's physical and emotional wellbeing. This addictive personality can then include abusing substances as the addict allows for such addictions. The thinking invites any and all addictions.

The addict maintains his behavior as he participates in denial. The ability to ask for help is difficult becomes most addicts think they can cure themselves. The reality is that addicts often need more than just saying to themselves that they can cure themselves based on will power. This is not enough for either type of addict. Addicts are more effective if they educate themselves on the path to change and follows all steps in this guide even if change is still slow to come. It may also be necessary to locate a therapist in your area. You have the ability to change addictive behavior but this includes hard work and dedication. Through dedication and knowledge you can change anything that is addictive in nature.

- WHAT BEHAVIORS DO YOU CATEGORIZE AS ADDICTIVE?
- HOW ARE YOUR BEHAVIORS SEXUALLY AND WITH SUBSTANCES/ALCOHOL THE SAME?
- WHAT WOULD YOU LIKE TO ADDRESS FIRST AND HOW DO YOU PLAN TO BEGIN YOUR PROCESS OF CHANGE?

Chapter Six

CHANGE AND SUCCESS

You determine if you are successful. You have to identify your behavior and the damage it is causing. Many times people begin the process of change and then lose their focus. Change IS hard work! You have to always continue learning about your sexual irresponsibility and its impact on others – this includes your sexual choices. Success comes with hard work, determination and an ability to consider others. Keep your goal in mind and take reasonable steps towards this change. When you feel discouraged look at why you feel discouraged. Hopelessness is possible because people lose the ability to put in the hard work and become complacent to their own urges. Some feel discouraged because the process can be a long one. Losing one's motivation is a problem in resolving addictive behavior. You have to remember that you are worth any difficult process. The benefit has to outweigh the cost! When you accept that your life will be improved by identifying behavior and changing it, then change can begin. Don't be discouraged! If your first try fails, then try again. Some behaviors have been in existence for years. It takes more than a few months to extinguish them. Your change results when you honestly want to eliminate a behavior, identify what is blocking change, learn your triggers, realize that you are worth any process, decide that you can make the changes that would benefit your life, see that achieving your goals changes your behavior, and finding change by eliminating high risk environments. You have to want change so badly that success is the only possibility. This may be a long road or a short one but failure is not an option!

Denial is a defense that you do not need! It breeds complacency and the ability to excuse your own actions that have always been at best inappropriate.

You can sabotage your own success by buying into denial. There are extensive barriers that prevent change and denial is one of these barriers. Other barriers may include justifying your behavior (I was drinking so I did something I otherwise would not have done sober) and minimizing your behavior (I didn't hurt her physically so my behavior is not that bad). You may have participated in these defenses for quite some time. They were no use then and they are no use now. If you really want change, then you have to look at why you continued behaving the same way. Most times change is not accomplished because you have blocked change with these defenses. Learn what your barriers are and begin to address them. Only with total acceptance comes change. Give yourself time to work through what has brought you to this information. Resign yourself to eliminating what is causing you shame and embarrassment. There are no short cuts to having healthy and positive relationships based on honesty and trust.

- WHAT DEFENSES ARE BLOCKING CHANGE?
- WHAT WILL BE KEY IN BEING A SUCCESS STORY?
- DO YOU THINK YOU HAVE THE ABILITY TO ELIMINATE YOUR SEXUAL BEHAVIOR?
- WHAT DO YOU THINK YOU NEED TO ELIMINATE IN ORDER TO BE SUCCESSFUL?

Chapter Seven

HIGH RISK ENVIRONMENTS

It is very important for you to identify and avoid high risk environments. This may include avoiding old habits such as peers that have dangerous thinking or environments that present an opportunity to resort to old behavior. For instance, if you were an addict, you would not associate with other addicts or use another drug to satisfy your cravings so that you don't use your drug of choice. In sexually inappropriate behavior, you must not engage in activities or environments that encourage past behavior. Sexual behavior is identical to drug addiction. For instance, you would not be an environment where there are children if your desires are for children. Purposely putting yourself in this environment is an invitation to have inappropriate thoughts.

If you engage in behavior telling yourself that you can control your thinking, this is destructive and avoids any new way of thinking because old habits may return. You have a choice as to whether you are in high risk or low risk environments. You can avoid for the most part any environments that lead to old thinking. If you are attracted to children, you would not be in a setting where children congregate. In reality you are putting yourself at risk each and every time you are in an environment where there are children. If you are attracted to adults, then you should do the same. Do not visit environments that are geared towards inappropriate thinking or behaviors. For instance, sometimes a person attracted to impulsive sexual activity will use prostitutes or random sexual partners they meet on social media to satisfy their urges. Even though this appears harmless, consider the possible risks and also the possibility that this will increase inappropriate thinking. The risks are the possibility of HIV, destroying a long term relationship, interference with your responsibilities (ie work), and legal issues if you are caught in an activity that is breaking the law. Don't excuse your behavior by thinking that some of these behaviors are not hurting anyone. For instance if you view child pornography, you perpetuate a market for this material because you are viewing it.

Often sexual behavior is fueled by the use of high risk environments that allow you to justify how your environments as harmless. Behavior exists because it is repeated. Often this is due to one participating in high risk environments. You must choose settings that perpetuate only healthy sexual choices.

Many addicts feel they are strong enough to be in high risk environments. This is seldom the case. You may think that you can participate in high risk environments and not be affected. In reality, anything we do or say is not done in a vacuum. You are creating an avenue to continue your inappropriate behavior. If you continue, then your efforts now may be in vain.

Do not allow for any excuses such as "I can quit anytime I want to". If you could you wouldn't need help for your behavior. These and other excuses lead to continuing a behavior that you find troubling. Only with total honesty with yourself and others will you experience genuine and healthy emotions.

Avoid any environment or setting where your behavior is acceptable or encourages it to continue. This offers a safer ground to build healthier sexual choices. Do not see environments as harmless because they are not.

- WHAT ARE THE HIGH RISK ENVIRONMENTS YOU SHOULD AVOID?
- WHAT EXCUSES DO YOU GIVE YOURSELF TO MAINTAIN SEXUAL BEHAVIOR YOU WISH TO STOP?
- WHAT COULD YOU DO TO STOP CREATING HIGH RISK ENVIRONMENTS DO YOU WISH TO AVOID AND WHAT WILL REPLACE THEM?

Chapter Eight

ACCOUNTABILITY

To change behavior, you first have to identify the sexual behavior you are participating in and your need to blame others (especially victims). Before you can change your behavior, you must be able to accept your role in it! You must admit to yourself that you are solely responsible for your sexual behavior and responsible for the damages that have stemmed from it. YOU MUST BE WILLING TO ACCEPT THAT YOU AND YOU ALONE HAVE THE COMPLETE AND TOTAL RESPONSIBILITY FOR A BEHAVIOR THAT IS NEGATIVE IN NATURE!

First you must be responsible for all your choices and able to take on the shame and embarrassment resulting from your behavior. Your sentences in speaking of your behavior should start with "I". Not "she" or "he". You are the creator of this behavior and responsible for all of its effects.

Often people with sexually negative behavior make excuses and they cause barriers that lead to frustration. You must be willing to take on all of the excuses you have used thus far and begin to not buy into these excuses any longer. Excuses such as these are never healthy: the victim wore provocative clothing, the abuse did not affect her, she was wanting the sexual encounter, everybody does sexually inappropriate acts and should not be held accountable because they happen all the time, or because you weren't arrested the behavior is not that bad. You cannot change a behavior that you feel you are not responsible for!

The first step is to own your choices, and identify ways to develop total and COMPLETE accountability. It is a painful process because you want to not be responsible for embarrassing and damaging behavior but this is the only way to change your sexual decisions. You must manage the shame that follows but still be willing to understand that your choices, however painful, through complete accountability.

People often find this step the most difficult. Nobody wants to have such a damaging behavior. It is easier to blame everyone else. Total accountability is the only way to eliminate a behavior. You MUST acknowledge any decision made from poor choices. You have to be accountable for you but also the effect on the people around you! You can only change what you acknowledge to be wrong. With accountability you can begin to accept your behavior and decide when and if you want to change it.

- IDENTIFY THE EMOTIONS THAT STEM FROM BEING TOTALLY ACCOUNTABLE?
- IDENTIFY THE BENEFITS OF TOTAL ACCOUNTABILITY.
- WHAT ARE YOU EXCUSES FOR DOING WHAT YOU DO?
- WHAT HAVE YOU DONE AND WHY ARE YOU RESPONSIBLE?

Chapter Nine

TRIGGERS

A trigger is something that leads you to indulge in your negative behavior. Triggers can often lead you to engaging in the behavior you claim you want to change. An example of this would be: You are an addict and are using heroin. You tell yourself you want to change but you do not throw away your needles, and eventually you use. The needles remind you of how badly you want to use and the way you felt when using. The needles act as a way to encourage your returning to the drug and a way to use your drug of choice.

The trigger associating with these needles help you use and encourage you to forget what resulted from this drug use. If you threw away these needles, this would be more consistent with change.

If you wish to see this sexual behavior as addictive (and some experts do), then you have to first name your triggers so that you can resolve them. Then you work diligently and frequently on avoiding such triggers. First, make a list of triggers that are specific to you. Triggers can include having sex with random partners or prostitutes, answering ads on social media, going to places where children play (if sex with children is your issue), engaging in sex with intoxicated individuals, viewing child pornography, exchanging sex for drugs, and thinking of women in derogatory ways or thinking less of them. Any of these can serve as a trigger. When you engage in these behaviors, then you increase your risk to yourself and others.

Your triggers act as a way to continue behavior that is a problem. When you identify them you are on your way to better sexual decisions. You should never participate in behavior that complicates or allows you to act sexually irresponsible. This is the most important step to changing your behavior. You must change your environment before you can change your thinking. It is often difficult to address triggers because you want the ability to say "it just happened" or "I just got caught up". The reality is that nothing just happens. Specifically, negative sexual behavior doesn't just happen and you participated in the environment that allowed you to continue this behavior.

Triggers are a way to continue to make excuses so that you can participate in the negative choices that have caused you trouble.   Excuses have no place in wanting to change your behavior. You have made excuses for yourself up to this point and this ended in failure. Now it is time to eliminate anything or anybody that leads to the same excuses and leads to triggers that lead to negative sexual behavior. Triggers can be a huge part of your recovery.

Note your triggers and how they affect your thinking. This will encourage success and the ability to avoid a behavior that has led you to this information

- WHAT ARE YOUR TRIGGERS?
- HOW CAN YOU AVOID THESE TRIGGERS?
- HOW READY ARE YOU TO IDENTIFY THESE TRIGGERS?
- WHAT DO YOU NEED TO DO TO ELIMINATE TRIGGERS THAT LEAD TO NEGATIVE SEXUAL CHOICES?

Chapter Ten

WHO DO YOU TELL

This question of "telling" is very different for everyone. For the most part, you should tell others that you feel have your best interest at heart. It is difficult to make this decision when this sexual behavior causes so much grief. Secrecy however is not your friend. You need to identify people who would support your need to change this behavior especially sexual partners. You should not expect to maintain this secrecy especially with present sexual partners. They need to have all of the information to make informed decisions about your relationship. Honesty and the ability to engage them in your process can be very helpful in deciding if you need to change your behavior. You have to decide who you will tell and when.

If you are already in a relationship, ask yourself if keeping your partner out of the loop really is beneficial for either of you. It is best to tell a partner even if you fear rejection. It is better to tell a partner and risk rejection then to be committing sexual acts behind their back. Secrecy has no place in a healthy relationship. It may cause great shame in the beginning and you may find that others can be judgmental but the alternative is that you are in a relationship that is not honest or healthy.

Partners often are willing to help if they are told early and in a productive way. You will not experience any support, if you wait years or months to engage their help. It is unhealthy for someone to learn of a sexual behavior that has gone on for many years. Remember sexual choices of any kind changes a relationship. Your fear of rejection can hold you hostage for a long time. If you can't be honest maybe you need to be in a place where your behavior only affects you.

Determine first who to tell and then when to tell. This is your process and that must be determined by you. Think of a plan to tell others of your present and your past. Imagine and possible responses by your partner. Then take on the responsibility of being honest especially of any thinking that affects your relationship.   You can't expect for someone to be in this process of change when they don't know the extent of your problem.   Think of ways to include them and how they can support your process. Always think of how to tell and what words you will use. Consider the response that you will get. The decision lands on your shoulders and it is up to you to decide how to tell. Never see your behavior as just your problem. If you are in a healthy relationship, then it is not just your problem. You have a responsibility to include your partner because the relationship is affected by other sexual behavior. Never assume that if they don't know, they are not affected. This is seldom the case!

- HOW WOULD YOU TELL A PARTNER ABOUT YOUR BEHAVIOR?
- DO YOU THINK HONESTY CAN BE AVOIDED DUE TO A FEAR OF REJECTION?

Chapter Eleven

BARRIERS AND THE ATTENTION TO SELF

Barriers to change must be eliminated early in your recovery. They at times are not always evident to the person working on change. It is your task to identify barriers and what part they play in your behavior. The need to identify them is very important in accomplishing change. Barriers act as deterrents for change and can be very troublesome. You must first have to accept that they are there and address them. To accept them, is to build a stronger foundation for change. You can eliminate their impact by identifying them early. This is necessary because change can be painful and intense. The impact of barriers is up to you. Ignoring them will cause a heavier impact than dealing with barriers head on.

Many reasons why people avoid change is because change is scarier than the continuation of negative behavior. The barriers to success are a large part of this process. Sometimes barriers are overwhelming at first. It is easier to accept your behavior without focusing on the barriers that prevent change. It is often amazing how long someone will maintain a bad behavior so that they do not have to change their thinking or be responsible for it. This is sometimes caused by a person ignoring their barriers which hinders progress. You may have continued to make the same mistakes irregardless of the consequences because not changing is easier. If you ignore the barriers and other obstacles you face, then change will be more difficult.

Another reason for not changing is the ability to achieve pleasure in something that is not beneficial to others. You have put your needs first and ignored how others are impacted by the behavior. Sexual disorders are often selfish and require that one be focused on only their own needs! Change dictates that the needs of others must be considered. Considering others on a sexual level is often difficult and may act as a barrier. You must always consider what blocks change and work on resolving this once and for all. You, however, at present are able to get your needs met and keep these barriers in place. It can be more rewarding (at least you think so) in maintaining barriers that do not allow for the sexually positive thinking.

A normal healthy relationship is based on give and take. It is often easier to participate in selfish behaviors and sexual gratification that leads to meeting your needs without considering others. Give and take is often a scary prospect. Recovery means that you have to consider someone else's needs. Having destructive sexual behavior is based on the need to totally focus on oneself. Common barriers may be: ability to lie to oneself about the gravity of one's behavior, a lack of motivation, a need to avoid sexual partners that require normal give and take, thinking that avoids taking into account the rights of others, and the lack of desire to form healthy relationships over one night stands, etc. Barriers prevent change by blocking out healthier choices. Often a barrier can feel insurmountable. Often that is not the case but it is experienced that way

Barriers are just barriers and can be overcome. You can cross over to real change by not allowing them to be stronger than your desire to change. A barrier is only as strong as the energy you give it. Your motivation to change can overshadow a barrier and it is often best to break down such a barrier even if it entails chipping away at its foundation. You have the power to decide if these barriers are something you can resolve or something that blocks your way

- WHAT ARE YOUR BARRIERS TO CHANGE?
- WHAT ARE THE TRUE BENEFITS BROUGHT ABOUT BY CHANGE AND THE RESOLUTION OF BARRIERS?
- WHAT EXCUSES HAVE YOU GIVEN TO MAINTAIN SEXUAL BEHAVIOR AND AVOID BARRIERS TO CHANGE IT?

Chapter Twelve

STRATEGIES TO CHANGE YOUR THINKING

You should first identify the behavior you wish to change and own this behavior. Meaning you and only you are responsible for your behavior or mistakes you have made. You have to first acknowledge your own reasons for perpetuating negative sexual thinking. When you acknowledge the total role you have in focusing only on your own needs, then change can happen.

First, actively identify environments that do not support your selfish behaviors and identify people that do not support old behaviors. You must surround yourself with people that support the best you and environments that only support healthy relationships. If you focus on negative influences that do not support change, then you minimize your chances of behaving differently. You are a product of your surroundings!

Eliminate triggers such as pornography, inappropriate partners, fetishes that are destructive etc. Identify and eliminate triggers completely.

Identify reasonable goals that you want to achieve. Do not make them too big to accomplish. Many people try to make goals that are not realistic and when they fail they go back to the behavior they want to eliminate. Do not make goals for instance of never engaging in any negative sexual but instead make goals that can successfully be accomplished.

Identify barriers to change and ways to eliminate them. Avoid excuses such as "my behavior isn't that bad" or "I am not hurting anyone but myself". Excuses will never allow you to change because you have made these same excuses over time and nothing has changed. If your thoughts include excuses, then it will interfere with your process.

Next, identify people who have positive sexual behavior and can exhibit positive thoughts relative to their sexual relationships. These persons may be in a positive relationship now or they hold women to a high standard out of mutual respect. Now that you want change, these peers can model what are healthy sexual boundaries. This peer group should have healthy sexual thinking. Associate yourself with others who respect their partners. Negative peers support bad behavior. You choose the models for healthy sexual behavior over having negative peers. Accept their input and use your knowledge to decide which relationships promote change. Negative influences or relationships breed negative results. You can then see the benefit of healthy relationships IF YOU MAKE CHOICES THAT RESPECT YOURSELF AS WELL AS OTHERS!

BE ACCOUNTABLE! In the end, you are responsible for your choices. By being accountable, you accept the blame and responsibility for your behavior. Accountability is the cornerstone to change and healthy thinking. You have to be accountable to really accept change and eventually must be accountable for your own mistakes. Nothing happens without accountability.

Identify other interests to act as distractions to replace temporarily the old interests that included irresponsible sexual choices. Other interests won't take the place of negative behavior but are helpful for a short time. Find positive activities where you can occupy your mind until you have achieved long term change. Positive activities eventually should replace activities that have brought you negative results.

Consider therapy if your behavior is severe enough to warrant such help. You can also locate Sexual Abusers Anonymous if available in your area. Read any literature about sexually negative behavior and learn more about this issue. Educating yourself is never a bad idea.

Identify people you have exploited when performing sexual acts. This is only in your mind as you should never face victims or partners you have harmed. Victims do not care about your apology. Let them address their damage and you address yours. You can write a letter to your victim but DO NOT mail this.

You may use journaling to better identify your poor choices and use your entries as a way to visibly see the mistakes that continue to occur. You have a chance to review your choices and see how your thinking results in poor choices. This acts as an activity where you can see any triggers that lead to negative behavior. You can see your perception of negative sexual behavior in your writing and you may find writing thoughts down can be a positive way to examine your own thinking.

Record any negative behavior. You can then look at your thoughts later. When a person is faced with their own writings it is often more helpful than some material on the market. You can evaluate your specific choices.

Remember your small achievements over time and reward yourself for such achievements. You deserve a reward to physically acknowledge your change in thinking.

Remember change is a process. Don't worry if you falter. Get right back up and continue your process. We are humans with the ability to make mistakes. Don't get caught up in your own failures. You should never chastise yourself for trying to engage in new behavior. Acknowledge the smaller changes you have made.

In conclusion, you need to follow these steps so that you are able to clarify the destructiveness of your behavior. It is often easier to look at a problem if you can break it down. This is very important because behavioral changes are often easier to implement then emotional changes. Look at the environment in which you exhibit this behavior and eliminate that environment! This is sometimes harder than it may seem at first. In reality, environments change when you change them! If you find yourself going to or indulging in high risk environments, you MUST change the environment to change the behavior! Don't make excuses for the decisions that result in the same choices. CHANGE YOUR ENVIRONMENT AND YOUR BEHAVIOR. ALSO ELIMINATE TRIGGERS AND ELIMINATE BAGGAGE THAT LEADS YOU TO FOCUS ON YOUR OWN SEXUAL SATISFACTION. OTHERS MATTER TOO!

You need to address the psychological impact of your choices and this can start with behavioral work. Triggers, barriers and environmental changes are part of your recovery. They are an important part of your recovery. These all have to be addressed over time. If you cannot dissolve such thinking, your process will be more difficult.

When this work is done, you can address changes needed for your emotional growth. Develop an emotional investment in your own recovery. Meaning that you are accountable and you want to change the way you think. You now have made a resolution to make healthier choices. Your emotional investment is what you are willing to give to make positive choices. The investment is your obligation to engage in positive behavior and what you will risk to have such change.

If for example you are viewing child pornography, first decide on how you can eliminate your use of pornography as a whole and maybe even the computer itself. Then identify the emotional benefit of this pornography. What are you gaining from this activity and what are you not gaining. You need to change this behavior before you experience relationship issues, job loss, or legal consequences. Your "emotional investment" has been in watching underage children engage in sex and achieving sexual gratification. You must prevent the immediate gratification that is gained by viewing pornography. This can be in replacing activities that are healthier. Find the emotional payoff from typical sexual activities and avoid negative triggers such as this. Do not allow yourself to think that child pornography is a harmless activity especially when sexual addiction exists. There are activities for you that are more significant than your average person. Porn can be one of these triggers.

Relative to goals, negative compulsive behavior prevents you from achieving your goals. Make goals reasonable. Your short goal may be to not engage in viewing pornography and then replace this activity immediately with something that brings you pleasure (this is not sexual but simply what you find enjoyable). Or your short term goal would be to abstain from using your computer and make other changes that you can implement easily. The use of limitations can be very helpful and lead to more self control. This gives an addict time to identify more and more serious behaviors that can be eliminated. The goal early in recovery is often to eliminate any impulsive sexual activity but eliminating the behavior altogether is often impossible. Your ability to avoid behavioral cues at first is more helpful such as avoiding ways to engage in pornography. You should pursue instead activities that bring you momentary pleasure.   Just eliminating the habit is not enough because eliminating such activities may be overwhelming.   First start with smaller goals to avoid any availability of porn and avoid the physical activity that you use to continue this activity. This ability to divert your attention may later lead to larger changes. Identifying the steps that you chose to make is a step in a positive direction.

A long term goal may be to abstain from any activity that promotes irresponsible sexual behavior. This long term goal would be to not engage in any sexual activity that leads to excessive use of pornography. This is a goal that is completed over time. This should be attempted later in your recovery. Start with short term goals first. Make achievable deadlines for yourself. Replace old stimulants with new healthier ways to have sexual gratification. Always consider the rights of others. Embark on a road to self discovery that will lead to change and avoids any negative impact on others. Take these steps in order to avoid negative sexual behaviors.

- WHAT STRATIGIES CAN YOU IDENTIFY TO INCREASE YOUR CHANCE OF SUCCESS
- WHAT IS A REASONBLE GOAL FOR YOUR CHANGE?
- WHAT SELF DISCOVERY DO YOU PLAN TO CHANGE?

Chapter Eleven

A PLAN FOR SEXUAL BOUNDARIES

Boundaries are a result of positive sexual thinking and become a source of displeasure for the sexual addict. This is difficult because you have worked to violate boundaries over time and now need to incorporate this misuse in your recovery. First you must accept that you have poor boundaries and as a result you violate the boundaries of others. By having negative sexual behavior, you may not aware of what healthy boundaries are. When you look at your emotional space then you do not allow for sexually inappropriate behavior. Your boundaries are lines you draw that no one should cross. Everyone has sexual boundaries, and if you are participating in negative behavior, you are most likely crossing someone's boundaries whether on line or in person. The person may not recognize that you are doing so but this does not mean it is not happening. You should never be willing to cross boundaries that intrudes on the space of others. You should focus on developing boundaries that have healthier repercussions. Develop boundaries that are solid and respectful of others. When you have healthier boundaries others will respect you for them. You start with recognizing the boundaries of others and what this means for you. Your new awareness of such boundaries creates a space where you respect other people.

You have probably violated your own idea of what you will and won't tolerate (and inappropriate sexual behavior as you see it.) Others have the right to their own beliefs and these should not be overshadowed by your own behavior. Everyone should respect their own boundaries in a healthy sexual relationship. When you begin considering others, then your partner's boundaries as well as yours will be respected.

To be successful in not violating the boundaries of others, you must identify which of your behaviors is not successful in honoring their boundaries. This can be a part of a healthy process. Make yourself a plan to move away from behavior that violates others' space. This is where your motivation is key. Motivation will determine how successful you are.   There is no shame in not achieving immediate results. There is only shame in quitting.

Overstepping one's boundaries starts with a promise to yourself to change the deeper emotions that are being used to have negative sexual behavior. When you move towards greater accountability you will learn appropriate sexual activities that encourage others to not feel violated. Your final goal is to have sexually interactive behavior without violating your partner's space. This is done as part of your changing perspective. When you have a healthy sexual relationship, you will find that both parties maintain their own boundaries.

When you begin to respect others you will find that proper boundaries are necessary for healthy relationships. Both partners should enjoy their emotional space and the result will be rewarding. When you don't violate others, they become more open to your sexual rules. You must examine whether your behavior benefits you but leaves others feeling very violated. In considering the rights of others, the ability to not evade their space will become natural.

- WHAT BENEFIT DO YOU GET FROM YOUR BEHAVIOR?
- WHAT ENVIRONNMENTS IN WHICH YOU ENGAGE IN ENCOURAGE NEGATIVE SEXUAL BEHAVIOR
- WHAT EMOTIONAL PAY OFFS TO NEGATIVE SEXUAL BEHAVIOR
- WHAT STEPS CAN YOU TAKE TO ADDRESS YOUR BEHAVIOR WITH LONG AND SHORT TERM GOALS?

Chapter Fourteen

IMPULSIVE THINKING

It may be difficult to accept that you have impulsive thinking in at least one area of your life. The word 'impulsive" sounds very insulting at first. It is actually a very common word that could in essence describe a behavior in everyone. In your case, we are using this to describe how you relate to sexual thoughts. Your impulsive thinking has continued to guide your sexual choices.

Impulsivity is the obsessive need to behave in a way that does not acknowledge the consequences. This includes sexual behavior. People who are impulsive make poor sexual choices. An impulsive person may eat a whole box of cookies and not concern themselves with the stomach ache. Sometimes people can be impulsive in several areas of their life. Sexually impulsive people engage in negative sexual behavior with little self control. They do not concern themselves at the time with who gets hurt. You can see yourself as having destructive sexual behavior without embracing the word "impulsive". This word just means that your brain works differently than someone else's. This can also be the case in using substances/alcohol or any other repetitive behavior. Impulsivity can be changed through acceptance and hard work. If you are offended by this label change can be a little more difficult. You have to accept that being impulsive is often the reason for your behavior and the common thread in why your behavior is exploitive and destructive

It is not productive to try to change behavior but ignore labels that you find unpleasant. You can change your thinking by accepting that your thinking is different than others especially in the area of sexual behavior. By accepting this label, you acknowledge that there is a problem and you want to change your behavior. It is not enough to want change and then be offended by the label.

Identify all impulsive behavior including sexual choices and how you would like to change these behaviors. Use the steps in previous chapters. Identify what parts of your behavior and your thinking that would be considered impulsive.

Impulsivity can be a very difficult word to accept. However you must accept that your thinking is different and not healthy. You may think of this as a character flaw without labeling yourself. The more you know yourself the better your chances of changing your thinking and behavior.

If you are impulsive then accept that and address change. With honesty, you begin to accept that your behavior is an issue. You can then embark on steps that address impulsive behavior and understand why you need to be motivated. By accepting that you have impulsive thinking, this is another step towards change.

WHAT BEHAVIORS WOULD BE CONSIDERED IMPULSIVE?

WHAT BEHAVIORS CAN YOU CHANGE THAT WOULD BE CONSIDERED IMPULSIVE?

Chapter Fifteen

PEDOPHILIA AND PARAPHILIA?

Therapists in general have a manual for diagnosing any disorder. This can be a scary process but it just allows one to really look at their symptoms and how they are categorized in the mental health field. Many people have diagnoses that do not define them as a person but simply defines their behavior. This is necessary so that a professional can define your symptoms and figure out how to help you. It can also be helpful in addressing your own behaviors.

Pedophilia means that you are sexually attracted to children. Although most people think of pedophilia is someone with a rain coat on trying to grab children as they walk by, it is simply an attraction to children (usually young children). The reality is that pedophiles are excited by many variations of child nudity and in reality do not have to actually touch or have sex with children. They may or may not have contact with a child. They use images of a child or actual contact with children to feed their sexual fantasies. A pedophile might use the internet to view child pornography and/or masturbate to these images. It may also include someone who fantasizes about children but doesn't actually touch them. If you find yourself attracted to young children or achieve sexual satisfaction by contact or by viewing images of children, then you would be considered a pedophile. This is a serious issue and must be addressed before any harm comes to children. If you are viewing images online of children you are feeding a market wherein real children are being exploited or abused.

A pedophile is anyone who sees children as sexual beings. The rule for a diagnosis of pedophilia is that you are sexually excited by any contact or image of a child. This is vastly different than paraphilia. Paraphilia is a "trash can" diagnosis meaning that a paraphilia can be ANYTHING inappropriate sexually and the particular behavior does not fit any category. In reality, paraphilia applies to anyone participating in abnormal sexual behavior. Paraphilias are behaviors that are sexual but do not qualify as pedophilia but are still a major problem.

This diagnosis would apply to any behavior that is dysfunctional and is not defined by pedophilia or other more specific names. Paraphilia can include rape of an adult or having compulsive sex, engaging in inappropriate sexual behavior (possibly with prostitutes). Any behavior in these categories is considered a problem. In making a diagnosis this is simply to describe your behavior and to better acquaint yourself with the label so that you can decide if this requires professional help. You can refer to the DSM-V if you want to read more on this subject.

- HOW WOULD YOU CLASSIFY YOUR BEHAVIOR?
- WHAT SYMPTOMS OR BEHAVIORS FALL INTO WHICH CATEGORY

Chapter Sixteen

GROOMING

The word grooming has a specific place in sexual addiction.   Grooming by definition is manipulating an individual into inappropriate sexual acts.   Examples would be to:

Give your victim a gift when your goal is to have sex with them.

Give your victim extra attention for sexually inappropriate acts.

Another example is to promise your victim anything that they will find valuable to interact with them sexually.

Anything a victim finds pleasurable can be seen as grooming. Your grooming is for the sole reason of gaining sex from an unwarranted partner. You offer gifts or attention to increase the odds that you will have sex with this person you are grooming.   Even if the manipulation seems less than purposeful it is just that. So that you can manipulate the victim into having sex with you. This increases their willingness to engage in sexually inappropriate behavior.   By the time you have asked for any kind of sex with them, you have used gifts or other objects as a way to gain control. You now have conditioned your victim to think of you in a positive light. You are the good guy – not the person who is preying on this victim. Grooming is calculated and deliberate. Now asking for sexual acts from the victim makes them feel obligated. Most times grooming is used to have sex with young victims and make them feel you are their friend. You have mapped out the path the abuse will take. Your grooming habits need to be examined and addressed. You cannot make positive changes without exploring your own thinking and the use of grooming. Sex should never be a negotiation between unequal (ie children) partners.

- AT HAVE YOU DONE THAT WOULD BE CATEGORIZED AS GROOMING
- WHAT GOALS HAVE YOU HAD THAT WOULD BE CONSIDERED GROOMING.

Chapter 17

COMPULSIVE IMPULSIVE THINKING

Both compulsive and impulsive behavior is difficult to change but possible with the right level of motivation. With these behaviors, thinking and behavior often exist regardless of the consequences. It may take several tries and a strong need to change. You must be stronger than the need to continue such behavior. Denial often is present which completely prevents one from changing such behavior. You have to know that your behavior is causing other problems and you have to be accountable for your behavior. You can't change something you refuse to believe is a problem.

Often with sexual compulsively, the behavior is destructive and repetitive. This can include compulsive sexual activity such as excessive masturbation or other addictions that lead to repeatedly engaging in activities that are having negative consequences in your life. This can be loss of relationship or loss of employment. As an addict, you probably repeat destructive behavior regardless of the aftermath. You may have compulsive behavior that has led you to have unnecessary risks to your sexual health. Sometimes you may have more than one addiction.

As an addict, you harm others as well as yourself. It is not enough to accept the labels that apply to destructive sexual behavior. You have to first admit to the addiction that is destroying your sense of what is appropriate and healthy. Look first at addictions that are the most immediate. You cannot end sexual impulsivity while you are in denial about alcoholism for example. All of your behaviors have to be addressed for you to change your life. It is not enough to want to change one behavior when other behaviors cause you serious consequences. If you think you have no other issues, then proceed to change your sexual thinking.

There are 12 step programs for just about any addiction. It would be helpful to identify what behaviors have caused you to experience negative thinking or behavior and gain support for any and all addictions. If you need support, 12 step groups are helpful.

Think about how you see sexual triggers and how best to address your thinking. You are the only person that knows whether you can conquer your impulsive thinking across many addictions. Any effort is better than no effort at all. It is better to embrace your impulsive thinking immediately rather than feel overwhelmed because you cannot find a starting point. Any work in this area can lead to long term change and you need to accept that your thinking is different than others. Don't allow yourself to be overwhelmed and first identify what your destructive behaviors are. Begin to address the addiction that is your sexual behavior and identify what sustains this behavior. You have maintained this behavior over time and everything that maintains this behavior has to be addressed eventually. That may be denial or justifying your thought process. You know what sustains this behavior. It is up to you to be honest with yourself and eliminate the excuses that creates such negative choices.

- WHAT ADDICTIONS DO YOU FEEL YOU HAVE?
- HOW DO YOU HOPE TO CONQUER ALL YOUR ADDICTIONS AND IN WHAT SETTING (12 STEP, THERAPY ETC.)?

Chapter 18

SHAME AND EMBARRESSMENT

People with inappropriate sexual behavior often find disclosing these behavior (or thinking about the behavior) very shameful. This sexual behavior takes on a kind of secrecy that people find the most disturbing in changing such behavior. People are often willing to keep this well hidden over actually changing this behavior. Shame can be powerful. Shame can be an overwhelming emotion and can lead to continuing problematic behavior that one finds shameful and embarrassing. The shame and embarrassment run so deep that changing it would mean dealing with these feelings. This can be scary! That alone can cause one to not address change. It is necessary however to really address a behavior without fearing the results. Embarrassment alone can be a deterrent for real change. When embarrassment or shame are present, there can be a fear of being vulnerable and exposing years of shameful behavior. Only you can conquer shame. It is often helpful to examine your behavior and identifying the role of shame in your recovery. Most likely shame when not addressed prevents change and an understanding of what is healthy sexual behavior. You have to be stronger than your shame! Many people want change but stop this process when the shame becomes uncomfortable. With growth comes these feelings. Only by experiencing them can you achieve real change. When these become uncomfortable, it becomes necessary to think through these emotions and know that the end result will be worth the negative feelings that you experience. To really have positive change you must face the feelings that accompany sexually deviant behavior. This means addressing your shame. It is uncomfortable to accept that you committed acts that damage others but it is a necessary component to change. Often people feel they have to hide their behavior because other people will judge them. This may be true but you are not changing for other people. With gradual change, comes the lessening of shame. When you face negative emotions, you begin to accept that they exist and can look at ways to change such emotions. These emotions will begin to decrease over time. Emotions are a deterrent if you give up when feeling them. Emotions have to be addressed over the time if true change is desired. Allow yourself to feel these emotions but not so much that it ends your process.

It is hard to face barriers inherent in being more responsible. You may need to find your will power and your motivation. You can change anything you wish to with the right attitude. You learn to want change in spite of your negative emotions and shame becomes less comfortable. Shame will not prevent change unless you allow it to.

Keep in mind, that most people with problematic behavior find that it is almost as hard to be honest with themselves as being honest with other people. Your fear may be that others will no longer accept you because of your secrets and you may not be able to accept yourself and how you think. No one wants to face complicated sexual issues. In reality there will be people who cannot accept this news. There will be times where you cannot resolve your own thinking. Find people that are your supporters – it's that simple. You have to let go of others who are not going to make this journey with you. Find who can support honesty and the beginning of a very long road. You have to change your own denial that stands in the way of change.

People with inappropriate thinking often have great difficulty at first accepting that they are suffering from sexually inappropriate thinking because it is so personal. They fear what they have done to others and even to themselves. Shame can be so powerful that continuing negative behavior is easier. This is a slow process and you want to acknowledge reasons for intense emotions. You may make excuses for your avoiding change. These are your emotions wanting to interfere with your process. Once you are honest with yourself, you begin to lessen the grip that shame provides. Emotions are part of this process!

People with different sexual thinking are often struggling with embarrassment and only until they dedicate their mind to the process do they withstand change.

It cannot always be on your terms. Deviant behavior is often changed through honesty and courage. To change your choices, you have to bear your soul. That is the only way to address secrets that you have buried.

You cannot "pretty it up" or minimize the details of your behavior. Change is not built on a shaky foundation. You have to accept that your behavior is harming you and possibly others in a way that breeds further damage. You have to start with acknowledging the ugliness that is the truth and dedicate this time to facing the shame so that you can get better and move on.

- WHAT BEHAVIOR THAT YOU WILL SHARE BRINGS YOU THE MOST SHAME?
- HOW DO YOU EXPERIENCE SHAME AND WHAT WILL REDUCE THE IMPACT OF SHAME?
- WHAT IS YOUR FEAR IN HOW OTHERS WILL REACT?
- WHAT WILL HELP REDUCE YOUR SHAME?

Chapter Nineteen

PORNOGRAPHY

In initiating more acceptable behavior, you have to accept that pornography may be a trigger for those with inappropriate behavior. This can mean that you continue to participate in behaviors that closely resemble the behavior you are trying to eliminate. If one is looking at pornography, there is a chance that this will trickle down to more unacceptable behaviors especially in fetish pornography or child pornography. In trying to view pornography less often, you may still have urges to view such material. If you are viewing child pornography you should know that this can lead to other inappropriate behavior. Pornography can act as a way to further justify your other behaviors. Pornography is often a trigger for more serious sexual behavior. Some people engaged in viewing pornography can isolate this and never indulge in more powerful sexual behavior. However this may not be the case for you. Pornography is another impulsive behavior that has no place in addressing change. YOU have to discover whether this is a trigger for YOU.

Pornography can be a gateway to behavior you wish to change. An example of this thinking is someone who continues to smoke marijuana but is trying to stop drinking. It is very real that one behavior escalates another behavior. You know if this is true of you. Don't allow other activities to threaten the behavior you want to stop!

Often viewing pornography is a compulsive activity and this becomes a problem when addressing other behavior. Because something is legal it doesn't mean that this is safe for you.

This pornography can be a dangerous slippery slope that people often use to satisfy their cravings for inappropriate behavior. Pornography is a dangerous habit for some. This becomes a way to indulge in unhealthy sexual thinking. If this is your way of indulging in inappropriate thinking you should eliminate such viewing. Eliminate any resource that leads to compulsive thinking.

Pornography is even more risky when the images are of children or contain images where people portray themselves as children. It is essential that you realistically look at this behavior and ask yourself whether this is an attempt to control inappropriate sexual behavior. In reality this never works! You have to be free and clear of ANY behavior that mirrors the one you hope to get rid of. If you feel more impulsive when viewing pornography there is nothing in this behavior that is harmless. Often pornography is marketed to those with inappropriate ideas and your viewing helps create a market for such material

In the end, pornography is not a victimless behavior. If you become addicted to pornography with images of children or teens, then there is a chance you are perpetuating abuse. (Children and young adults in this environment are real people). Consider the images you view. Any pornography with inappropriate images is marketed to those with sexual impulsivity.

Triggers in general need to be avoided. In giving into something that is sexually provocative this can lead to behavior that you hope to change. Don't minimize pornography if this is a trigger for you.

- WHAT IMPACT DOES PORNOGRAPHY HAVE FOR YOU AND IS IT A TRIGGER FOR OTHER BEHAVIOR?
- WHAT ARE YOUR BEHAVIORS WHEN OR AFTER VIEWING PORNOGRAPHY?
- DO YOU ENGAGE IN VIEWING PORNOGRAPHY THAT REPRESENTS INAPPROPRIATE BEHAVIOR OR INAPPROPRIATE IMAGES?
- WHAT IS THE PURPOSE OF LOOKING AT PORNOGRAPHY?

Chapter Twenty

VICTIMS

Are there victims of your sexual behavior or is this a behavior that is only a problem for you. You know the answer to this question. You have to be honest in evaluating whether you have left victims behind.

In the case of victims whether by your hand or others, the damage is life changing. Victims of any sexual behavior are left wounded souls and become damaged over time. Victims are blameless and this must be accepted as fact. Don't blame for instance a teen for "lying about her age". In reality you initiate sexual encounters that are governed by your world experience. You are not on the same level as a teen. There is often manipulation that goes along with having sex with such young partners. You have to change the way you see this interaction. The age difference dictates that you are making harmful sexual decisions and manipulating situations that lead to inappropriate behavior. This is true of any behavior that you indulge in by coercing someone else. The person or child being targeted by your ability to manipulate other's sexual choices is a problem! They do not have your life experience or your level of maturity. You have the upper hand and any interaction with them should never be sexual.

Victims do not create their own abuse! They are the pawns in a situation where you seek them out and use their vulnerability to have this sexual encounter. This is a hard pill to swallow but is true. You have the upper hand in having sex with these victims.

If your sexual addiction involves any person that is a minor, then you are solely responsible. Don't look to others for the reasons why this occurred. Don't look to victims for reasons for the sexual encounter. They are the vulnerable one in these situations. If you have to manipulate someone or something this suggests that you are victimizing others. No one should ever have sexual encounters where a child is involved or depicted in child pornography.

Victims have damage over their lifetime as a result of their perpetrator's inappropriate behavior. You do not come first in any sexual interaction nor can you ignore the pain to others. A sexual encounter should be mutually beneficial and a positive experience for both partners. If this is not true, then there is a problem in the sexual encounters you create. As you begin to change your thinking, you will become more aware of who you have hurt. Even if this damage is only to yourself, then you should examine why these behaviors persist.

A word about the aftermath of your behavior - Victims work on their own recovery after having inappropriate acts with adults. This can be a very long path for them and their self esteem is most of the time what is affected the most. Victims do not want your apology or your sympathy as they pursue their own journey. Do not try to ease your conscience by engaging in discussions with the people you have harmed. They don't need anything from you! Your actions should be addressed within yourself. The damage is done and you can't fix that now by opening wounds that others have as a result of your behavior.

In reality you have to decide if you are harming others and how to stop such behavior. You have to focus on yourself so that you harm no one. However the damage to others should be part of your recovery. This recovery has to only involve you. Never approach a victim to ease your conscience.

Don't attribute any of your decisions to others. Ask yourself if you are negatively impacting someone's life or if this damage is part of your own poor selfesteem.

Don't focus on the victim's wellbeing and simply focus on your own wellbeing. They have their own work to do. Your intrusion on their process is damaging and will only interfere with their process.

A person hurt by your behavior should not be your focus. You have to heal yourself and allow others to heal themselves. Victims have a healing process that does not include your interacting with them. They are already damaged by your behavior and no further contact should be warranted. You have to focus on your own change and let victims focus on theirs. There is nothing to say that will make this better so don't try to apologize for your actions. Forgiveness is not for you to seek out.

Victims and the person engaging in questionable practices need to focus on resolving their own distorted sense of sexual practices. You should focus on your own psychological scars. You need to address the origin of your dysfunctional thinking. You have intense emotions to resolve and this should be the place to start. Your energy should be used to understand why you are able to justify having sex with inappropriate partners or harmful sexual choices.

Work on yourself and you will respect the victim more than any actual interactions. Focus on you!

- HOW DO YOU IMPACT OTHERS WHEN PRACTICING YOUR INAPPROPRIATE BEHAVIORS?
- DO YOU HAVE VICTIMS AND WHAT WOULD YOU SAY TO THEM?
- WHAT PSYCHOLOGICAL SCARS DO YOU HAVE DUE TO YOUR INAPPROPRIATE BEHAVIOR?

Chapter Twenty Two

WHY ME?

People who are faced with this idea of "why me" often use this as a way to not focus on what is important. Your sexual dysfunction is a result of your lifetime experiences. Whether this is fair or not, you are experiencing sexual dysfunction and it doesn't matter whether this is fair. You may feel that it is unfair that you have such destructive behavior. In reality, there is no trying to make sense of something that makes no sense. This is just the luck of the draw and there is no reason for you being the person with such poor judgment. Worrying about whether this is fair is a way to waste time and experience self pity. Everyone has adversity of some kind. You have to begin the process acknowledging that everyone has their own type of adversity.

There are no quick answers and wanting to identify the reasons for this dysfunction does not promote change. This thinking will slow down your ability to resolve behaviors because you have now become focused on what is fair and unfair. This is not productive!

To overcome behaviors that lead to dysfunctional behavior and harm to others, you have to accept that you have inappropriate behavior. The reason is not important.   One has to accept one's fate in order to change it. Many people suffer worse fates and overcome significant barriers. This is your cross to bear!

You have to initiate change with the idea that you can change how you behave and how you think. Sexual behavior has been present for a very long time – sometimes in early childhood. It can however be overcome so that your behavior harms no one including yourself. If you agree that you need to address your thinking, then change will be possible.   You have to want to change more than you want to stay the same and this means that YOU are sexually inappropriate or sexually addicted. You have to address change without evaluating who has this adversity.   You have to want change so badly that you do not divulge in self pity. Your pride and ego sometimes offers people excuses that are not valid or necessary. You first have to decide that what you are doing is harmful and then proceed from there. Denial is no one's friend and has no place in change. With change, comes a better understanding of who you are and not someone to be pitied.

If you have decided it is worth your time to look at your behavior, don't now justify the very behavior that brought you to this point. Change is hard but often is rewarding and necessary! When you accept that this problem is particular to you, then you can begin to focus on change. And whether you like the cards you were dealt is unimportant. Do not let a behavior define you!!! If you want to change, anything can happen. You have to own it and move towards better decisions. Your cross becomes lighter once you understand your own choices. The reason for who has what cross to bear is not important to the process ahead of you.

- DO YOU ENGAGE IN THIS "WHY ME" THINKING?
- WHAT THOUGHT PROCESS FOLLOWS SELF PITY?
- ARE YOU WILLING TO TAKE CREDIT FOR YOUR BEHAVIOR AND ABANDON SELF PITY?

Chapter Twenty Three

STARTING OVER

You can make a fresh start from any kind of adversity. You can be the person that you wish to be and not the person holding you back. You have to however admit to your behavior and make the changes necessary. The process may be seen as starting over because you have to make significant changes and this can resemble starting over. Do so with conviction and with an open mind. The first step is to admit to your inappropriate behavior and acknowledge that your behavior is not benefitting you. You have to be honest with yourself and those who you are deceiving. You must not invest in denial or other means that compromise your ability to change. You should never look at change as insurmountable because change in possible. Take these steps slowly and decide what is particular to you. When you are honest with yourself then everything else is possible. You have to make your own fresh start. If you are willing to face your issues than you face possible solutions. You are not above starting over because you deserve the results. Negative sexual behavior is a barrier to change but having a fresh start may entertain better relationships. Your start can involve a new perspective. When you start over in the way you think sexually then this leaves room for a fresh start

In the end, the only barrier to change is you! You have the ability to change and be happy. Starting over can involve healthier thinking and a promise to harm no one. You have to accept the need for change and see a fresh start as an emotional journey that only you can take.

Have relationships only if they are honest and healthy to both partners as part of your fresh start. When you make better decisions, you will have better relationships. Then this start becomes meaningful. The problem and the solution lies with you. Only through self acceptance do you see the need for change. The eventual acceptance of self can be rewarding but only if you are not behaving in a way that leads to negative choices. Through this process, you can create the idea that you are starting over emotionally and sexually in order to begin a more positive way of life.

Make this your own fresh start!

Chapter Twenty Four

ISOLATION

The first obstacle is to decide who you will tell and under what circumstances. Tell others first that you think would be nonjudgmental and able to support you in the change process. It is very difficult to know who to tell or whether to tell at all. This is often necessary if you want to be free of secrets and want support as you address your behavior. Identical to an addict, telling gains you support from your friends or relatives. It is uncomfortable because your issues are sexual, but you know who can support this process. Don't waste extensive periods of time to telling others who will not support this process – allow yourself to distance yourself from these persons. Tell the people who may support you and your process. Your sexual partner should be your first consideration because you are not being honest as part of this relationship. Partners need honesty!

If you isolate yourself completely this could lead to further shame and embarrassment. When you isolate yourself especially in order to not be honest then you can experience more and more excuses for your behavior. You have to decide how you choose to be honest but isolating yourself is not a chosen method to overcome shame. As part of your process, you will need to decrease your need to pull back and keep your behaviors as part of your secrecy. Negative behavior and isolation only creates more secrecy and derails your ability to change. If you are isolating in order to avoid involving others in your process that is a choice but doing so as a way to eliminate your behavior may be counterproductive.

When you chance telling someone about your sexual behavior, there is always a possibility that your disclosures won't be well received but this should not deter you. You can't use this as an excuse to continue to function in secrecy. A relationship has to be inclusive of mutual respect and honest emotions.   Sex is often a taboo subject. There is always a chance that your disclosures will lead to negative outcomes but discussing this cannot be off limits.   In the end, you have to focus on having positive sexual interactions regardless of the possible repercussions.   Don't let anyone stop your process. Secrecy hinders your progress because you are not receiving the support you need. You have to be your own source of support as well.   In the end, you have to maintain only honest relationships if you are to be successful.

Deceitful behavior has no place in any sexual relationship

- IN WHAT WAYS HAVE YOU BEEN DECEITFUL IN A SEXUAL RELATIONSHIP?
- WHAT QUALITIES DO YOU HOPE TO CHANGE AS YOU SEEK A HEALTHY SEXUAL RELATIONSHIP
- HOW DO YOU ISOLATE YOURSELF IN A UNHEALTHY WAY?
- HOW DO YOU HOPE TO CHANGE IN HOW YOU ISOLATE YOURSELF?

Chapter Twenty Five

HEALTHY SEXUAL RELATIONSHIPS

Sexual relationships are based on trust! This trust is difficult to develop when there is a history of trauma and/or sexually inappropriate behavior. Your past is always a result of whatever sexual thoughts you have ingrained in your mind. Often an inability to have sexually healthy relationships can be due to numerous experiences in your earlier life.   You may not have an idea of what a healthy relationship is or you may never have seen healthy relationships modeled for you. When you are trying to change your behavior, healthy relationships need to be part of this new way of thinking. You have to change how you see your sexual partners – specifically in respecting others. This is not to look for excuses. You can't hide behind "this is in the past" to develop relationships built on honesty. You must accept that you need to be honest with others so they can be more honest with you. When you respect yourself or others, sexually positive relationships will follow. However you can't respect others if the relationship is based on secrecy.   You must at some point trust your partner with information so they can make healthy decisions. These should not be based on a façade that prevents complete self exposure. They have a right to know! Then you can work together to build a relationship with a solid foundation.

You cannot hide your past if you hope to have a healthy relationship. You have to trust in others with your past even when that person's trust is being tested. You need to tell at your own pace but not so late that your partner feels that there has been this huge secret. Partners need to know you and your impulsive thinking. Partners should always be aware of what is in someone's "closet". Honesty should always be your remedy when trust is being tested. Those who stay have evaluated their choices and decide to leave or stay.   Lying builds a shaky foundation that ruins whatever relationship there could have been. You have to make important decisions in order to build a healthy relationship. People that love their partner are often willing to work with them to build healthier relationships. Don't decide for someone whether to share your past or not share your past. This is not fair to others!

Partners need to have all the information! This allows them the opportunity to decide if they chose to deal with your real character.   It allows them to consider what impact your sexual behavior has on them. Some may respect your honesty and therefore stay in the relationship while others will choose to leave. It is quite painful for a partner to find out about your behavior later in a serious relationship. They will feel that you have lied to them and this is unforgivable. Timing is everything. Tell others before they feel you have put on a superficial front that is hiding secrets. No relationship can be built on such secrecy.

You have to accept that there will be partners who choose to leave the relationship. That should not result in manipulating the feelings of others. You should still be honest because their decision is theirs to make. You will have to accept that there will be others who choose that they cannot tolerate a relationship with someone who has had negative sexual behavior. This is their right. You may need to move on and find someone who is willing to accept you and your baggage.   Honesty is everything! It will be difficult for others to accept your sexual decisions but there are no other ways to cultivate a healthy relationship.

Through hard work and time, you will begin to see your partner become more receptive to your disclosure.   You have to accept that some persons are not comfortable with your behavior. These persons and their response to you should be accepted and you should respect their response. Partners will need to examine their own feelings regarding your behavior. If you can't be honest with these partners it is best to not participate in a relationship at that time.   It is important to gauge when to tell so that you do not violate their sense of trust. This is decided solely by you. Do not decide merely based on your own convenience. Trust needs to be built early. Don't disclose and count on someone to being tolerant of this situation. People are different and the possibility exists that someone will not chose to tolerate a complicated relationship. Before entering into a healthy relationship know that you have been honest and forthcoming. If the relationship does not last past your disclosures, then the relationship was not as strong as necessary to survive your sexual past.   You always take a chance when disclosing any type of sexual behavior that another finds this too serious to tolerate!

Start working on your issues and then work towards greater honesty in disclosing your past to a sexual partner. Start earning trust by being honest and evaluating a partner's commitment. Decide when to disclose through evaluating the partner's dedication to you. Waiting too long can have lasting effects. In the case of sexual behavior, it is key to decide when and how to tell your secrets.

- WHAT HAVE YOU DONE TO END RELATIONSHIPS AND HOW CAN YOU CHANGE THIS?
- AT WHAT POINT TO YOU DISCLOSE AND WHAT WOULD BE A HEALTHIER EXCHANGE TO ENSURE THAT YOUR RELATIONSHIPS HAVE A BETTER CHANCE OF SURVIVING.

Chapter Twenty Six

LIVING YOUR LIFE

As you live your life, you will need to make important decisions that require change. This includes your sexual choices. These sexual choices now impact all areas of your life. Make a goal, especially important in eliminating negative behavior, and take steps toward this realistic goal. Remain focused even if you fail at first. Remember how your behavior affects others. Always maintain a focus on the impact of your behavior. Decide if you can live your life based on mutual respect and honesty. Don't put your needs first because this breeds self pity. If you are in a relationship, participate in total trust and honesty. Don't use others to fulfill your needs while hiding secrets from them.   Never be in a relationship where your behaviors are hidden behind a façade that you present to the world.   Address whatever negative sexual behavior you continue to practice and learn new ways to address this behavior. Identify all triggers that lead to such behavior and implement safer practices. Keep your goals in mind and develop ways to attain them. Believe in your own worth and allow yourself to participate only in healthy sexual behaviors. Work on any issues relative to poor self esteem. You deserve the positive result of appropriate sexual choices.

Be honest! To change, you must have examined your behavior and found strategies that help eliminate this over time. Have attainable goals and only associate with those who would not tolerate such behavior. You must build a positive support system and learn to associate only with positive forces in your life. Learn what keeps a negative behavior in place and change those triggers so that you have the best chance of change.

Try to move away from excuses such as: I am not really hurting anyone, I will tell everyone in my life eventually, I don't have the time to address my issues or others have more harmful behavior than I do.   These excuses may even have a ring of truth but the reality is that your behavior effects everyone including yourself. You will lack genuine relationships if you hide behind an appearance that is based on secrecy.

Identify people that make you feel worthy of a positive relationship. If others add to your lack of selfesteem this is harmful.   Eliminate people that encourage impulsive sexual behavior or participate in such behavior. You are who you associate with. Keep a stable and healthy support system that knows your past but is willing to work with you to eliminate the behavior you have identified.

Form only healthy relationships based on honesty. No one should be creating a relationship with you and they do not know your past. They deserve to make this decision without discovering later on that your behavior has been your negative and inappropriate. If you are prepared to be honest you may be ready for a healthy relationship. No relationship is positive if it is based on a façade.

Do not set up environments that encourage your negative behavior. For example, if you find you attracted to children, then do not visit areas where children congregate. Don't make excuses to be in environments that encourage impulsive behavior. Excuses have no place in a positive lifestyle.

Be as diligent in protecting others relative to your behavior as you are at protecting yourself. Treat others with respect.

You can build a life and still work on being an honest person. Often dealing with change is overwhelming but nothing can substitute for these steps. Find ways to avoid what can lead to this behavior. You have to prevent risks where you find them. Don't be afraid to leave environments that trigger inappropriate thoughts.

Find ways to improve your self esteem and/or end problematic behavior. This can be sharing with family your struggle, a support group or church, or a set of friends that love you no matter what. If you fall into the trap of self loathing you will not be successful. You are worth finding ways to improve your life and rid behaviors that you will only find shameful. Shame can be difficult to conquer but with the right decisions you can minimize this and move on. Everything seems overwhelming at first but you can move past your own denial and move to being a positive person.

Keep in mind that continuing this behavior is not an option. You cannot expect any support if you continue to make the same mistakes. You have to be totally committed to change before others can learn to accept and support you. If you continue the behavior and don't dedicate yourself to change, then you will not see the successes as they occur.   No one should support you if you continue to repeat negative behavior.   When you learn that change is possible, then others will see change as possible as well. You must develop with or without the help of others a plan that supports healthy behavior.

Chapter Twenty Seven

HONESTY VS. DECEITFUL BEHAVIOR

You have the capacity to be honest. Being deceitful is deliberate whether due to shame, embarrassment or resistance. Healthy relationships are formed with honest interactions. You have the right to be what you are but do not include others in your faulty thinking. People react to you as you behave towards them. It is not beneficial to live by deceiving others. With sufficient motivation you can change how you relate to others. When the behavior is gone so will be your need to justify the behavior. A person determines in their own mindset whether they are deceitful or honest. Your life is your decision. You can choose to build better relationships through not engaging in sexual behavior that is harmful. You decide if you wish to be honest or deceitful. You decide every day whether you respond deceitfully to others. Honesty is important! That is why it is important to have relationships based on mutual acceptance. You determine the level of honesty you have with others. When feeling the need to be deceitful, it is up to you to make the harder choices. You determine whether you are being deceitful or honest. Shame does not have a place in honesty unless you create relationships on shaky foundations. The reality is that you choose which relationships support your journey. This is especially important in romantic relationships. You can't have an honest sexual relationship if you find that your thinking has not changed.

In the end it is up to you to ask yourself when you become honest and with whom you become honest. The payoff to being completely honest can be negative at first but you build up your own ability to practice healthy interactions.

People may be angry at first but you will be practicing how to avoid secrets and unhealthy social interactions. Secrecy breeds poor self esteem and this leads to negative sexual relationships. You first have to ask yourself when and how you disclose – and this skill becomes more effective after practicing honesty in various relationships. Sometimes deceit is easier but it is only beneficial for a short time.

Make honest choices and learn to interact in a way that is not deceitful. You control your responses and interactions with others.

- HOW DOES YOUR DECEIT SABATOGE A HEALTHY RELATIONSHIP?
- HOW WILL PRACTICING HONESTY CHANGE HOW YOU PARTICIPATE IN A RELATIONSHIP?
- HOW WILL DISCLOSING PARTS OF YOUR LIFE IMPACT HOW YOU GAIN TRUST AND FORGIVENESS?

Chapter Twenty Eight

MAKING AMENDS

You have to consider after you have made significant changes to consider the need to make amends. This is not easy but necessary for certain situations. People in your life who have been impacted should be your focus after you fix your own thinking and behavior. You should never however focus on a victim. They have their own process. It is not for you to decide on their plan. You should never interact with others so that you feel better! You cannot ask others for forgiveness before you have been honest with yourself. Others in your life will decide how to heal their souls and you are responsible for healing your own.

Making amends comes from honest and complete change. Your ability to interact with others in a more honest way is the beginning of this process. Don't expect some persons to be receptive after you have hurt them. You can't convince anyone that you have changed unless they are willing to listen.

When you make amends do not do this for others. The first step is just knowing you have affected others. Others do not have to accept change just because you have done so. Others may by convinced you have changed while others feel you are looking for self pity. The best evidence is changing the way you think and behave. This shows others that you are serious about changing your impact on others.

Never reach out to victims to be a part of your process. Your process is only for you to pursue and never access victims. Your apologies are not for your victim. They are beneficial to you. Write a letter to your victim. Do NOT mail this. Use this exercise to process how you see your behavior. APOLIGIES HAVE NO PLACE IN SEXUALLY ABUSING ANOTHER PERSON. Focus on the reasons for your sexual behavior over the baggage left to most victims.

- HOW WILL YOU MAKE AMENDS WITHOUT USING VICTIM TO ACCOMPLISH THIS GOAL?

Chapter Twenty Nine

Conclusion

It is possible that your sexual thinking and correcting this thinking is a very long process. People often get frustrated by the insurmountable task of changing what they have always done. Now is the time however to put old excuses to bed. You have to engage in this process if you want to eliminate behavior that has caused you significant problems. There are no easy solutions. But you can allow your motivation to replace your sexual shame. The only way to change anything is by first acknowledging this behavior and then by doing the work necessary to change it. Pain, shame and embarrassment have to be addressed diligently and head on. It is not enough to want your thinking to be different. You have to physically and emotionally change your thinking and your behavior. When you are honest with yourself then you can be honest with others. You have to face the reality that no journey is easy and without hard work. You can do what you allow yourself to do!!!!!!

If you fail, try again. Not everyone is successful the first time. You owe it to yourself to be responsible for your behavior as well as the changes that you need to make

Finally, do not let your behavior or your thinking to define you as a person. You are not a bad person but you practice bad behavior. Your behavior can be changed if you are motivated to change it. When you have conquered negative behavior you will be more motivated to continue your journey. Do these steps for you – not anyone else. Do not embrace the idea that change is easy! It is not. You haven't created these negative choices in a day so you won't be able to extinguish them in a day. Change takes time and motivation so you will need to allow yourself sufficient time to change but not so much time that you allow yourself to continue this behavior. You are your own supporter or your own worst enemy. Change starts with you and ends with you. If you want change badly enough it will happen. If you make excuses for bad behavior then you will not be successful in making significant changes.   Take the first step by identifying what your addictions are and what you would like to change. It is overwhelming at times to conquer multiple addictions but with the right attitude and need to replace denial you can end old thought patterns. Nothing is ever impossible unless you make it impossible. Be honest with yourself and start today to resolve what has led you pain and embarrassment.   Then let change happen!

USE THESE QUESTIONS TO REALLY ADDRESS BEHAVIOR THAT YOU MAY NOT HAVE CONSIDERED IN THE PAST TO BE A PROBLEM. HONESTLY ENGAGE IN RESPONSES TO EACH CHAPTER AND YOU WILL FIND YOURSELF ON THE ROAD TO SUCCESS WITH THE RIGHT MOTIVATION AND WILL POWER.